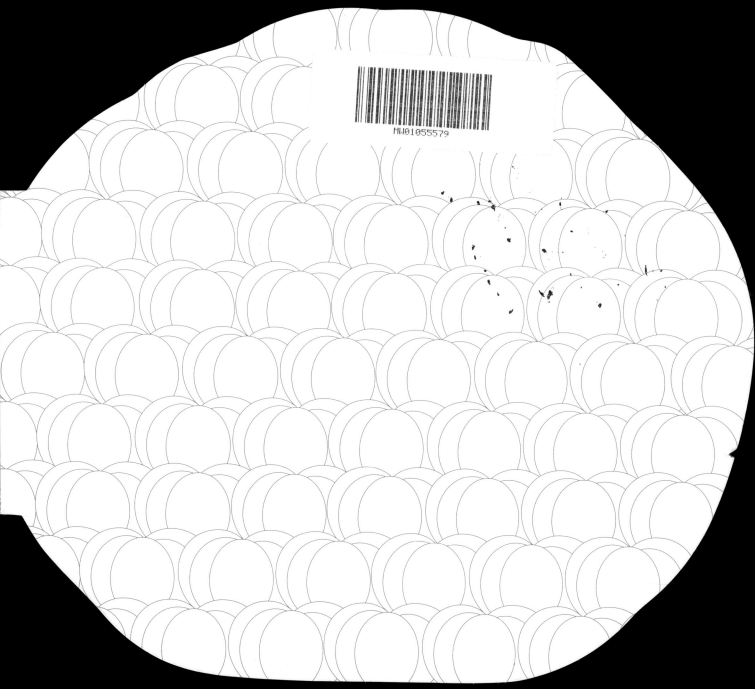

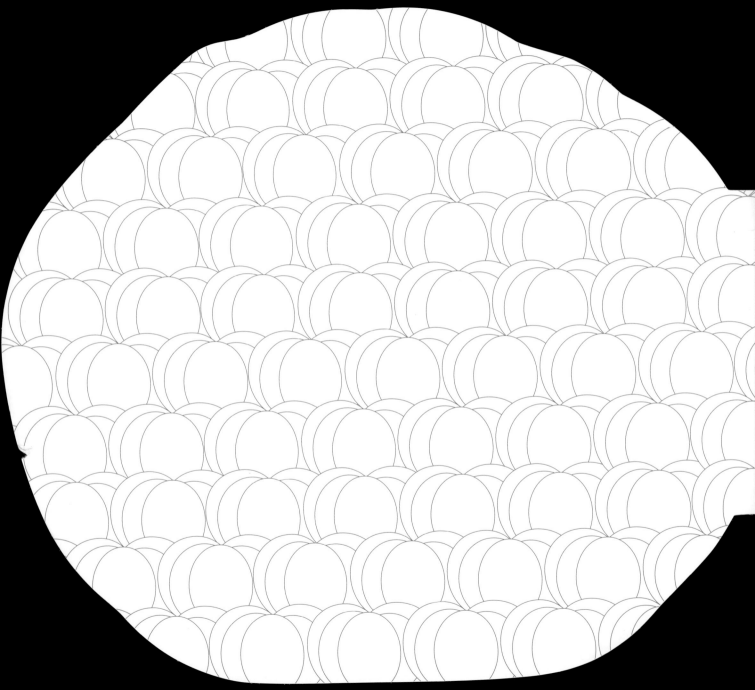

PUMPKINS

50 Easy Recipes

CREATED BY
ACADEMIA BARILLA

PHOTOGRAPHY
ALBERTO ROSSI
CHEF LUCA ZANGA

RECIPES
CHEF MARIO GRAZIA

TEXT
MARIAGRAZIA VILLA

DESIGN
MARINELLA DEBERNARDI

COORDINATION WITH ACADEMIA BARILLA
CHATO MORANDI
ILARIA ROSSI
REBECCA PICKRELL

CONTENTS

THE PUMPKIN?
SIMPLY MAGICAL

*"I think the first thing
you'll need is a pumpkin."*
The Fairy Godmother to Cinderella, in the fairy tale by Charles Perrault

It's a vegetable like no other. Not surprisingly, it's the universal symbol of Halloween, the holiday harking back to an old Celtic ritual that celebrated the communion with the spirits of the afterlife. We are used to seeing its surface carved into a toothless, grinning face, often with a flickering candle inside to ward off witches and ghosts. But the pumpkin's allure doesn't end here. Filled with countless seeds, it has, since antiquity, been regarded in the West as in the East as a symbol of the resurrection of the dead – who lie underground, like seeds ready to germinate – and as a halfway point for their ascent to Heaven.

Available in summer and in winter, carved out or full of flesh, ornamental or edible, their versatility is staggering: sweet, but not fattening, low in calories, but filling. Perfectly adapted for cooking, but equally useful in cosmetics and medicine, the pumpkin is simply magical.

A Mysterious Birth

If you need more proof that the pumpkin is not your usual garden produce, here it is: its birth is shrouded in mystery. The word pumpkin originates from the word pepon, Greek for "large melon". The French adapted this word to pompon, which the British changed to pumpion and later American colonists changed that to the word we use today, "pumpkin".

Where does it come from? Better yet, where do they come from, since a great variety exists in every country in the world? Certain ancient populations, like Egyptians,

Romans, Greek and Arabs had and cultivated various kinds of pumpkins, probably imported from southern Asia. They also used them for other things besides food. In Rome, for example, pumpkins were appreciated at the table (the chef Apicio gave around 10 recipes in his *De Re Conquinaria*), but they were also used, once emptied of their pulp and dried, as light, waterproof containers for transporting salt and wine, milk or grains. Depending on the form and size, some pumpkins were also used to make plates, bowls, spoons and even musical instruments.

Native Americans also cultivated this vegetable: Christopher Columbus brought a few varieties back to Europe, the same ones that we still enjoy today, larger than the ones that had been consumed in European kitchens until that time. Although the oldest pumpkin seeds, dating back to 7000-6000 B.C., have been found in Mexico, we still are not certain that this edible plant is originally from Central America. In fact, according to some, it comes from India.

An Extended Family

The pumpkin belongs to the great Cucurbitacee family that also includes cucumbers and watermelons. It's an enormous family, counting over 90 genres and 900 species, large or small, oblong, twisted or round, smooth or wrinkled, ribbed or bumpy, green, yellow or striped. How many pumpkin varieties are there? Those most used in the kitchen belong to the Cucurbita Maxima species, in Italy called "Marina di Chioggia", round and turned in at the ends, with a hard and wrinkly rind that goes from grey to green with a sweet, grainy yellow-orange pulp, and the "Americana Tonda", round with a yellow rind ribbed with green and a flavorful, yellow-orange pulp. There is also the Cucurbita Moschata species, know also as the "Long of Naples", that looks like a club and can grow to be a meter long, with a

rind that varies from rusty red to orange with soft and very sweet yellow pulp.

Pumpkins, ripe in August and found on the market all winter, are not only varied in color in ever-changing forms and quickly developed (so quickly that often they are figured in art as the symbol of the fugacity of human life, like in Albrecht Dürer's "Saint Jerome in His Study"), but also constantly growing: some non-edible pumpkins, if they are not harvested at the right time, can grow to over 220 lbs. (100 kilos). In once case, the Guinness World Record was awarded to a pumpkin that reached 1, 100 lbs. (500 kilos)... This might be why, in Charles Perrault's famous *Cinderella*, the fairy uses a pumpkin, the largest pumpkin in the garden, to make the carriage that takes Cinderella to the ball!

Prodigious Virtues

Pumpkins are sweet, but don't be fooled: the pulp is actually low in sugar and rich in water (94%), thus favoring the body's purification. It is also particularly rich in antioxidants, vitamins – especially vitamin A, like all orange vegetables, and vitamin C – and minerals, above all potassium, phosphorus, calcium and magnesium. Thanks to its low caloric value, with only 15 calories for every 3 1/2 oz. (100 grams), its good fiber content and a highly satisfying flavor, it is ideal for those who follow a strict diet. Clearly, served with butter and Parmigiano Reggiano it is even more exquisite, but a bit higher in calories. Pumpkins are also a valid and flavorful "medical facilitator", able to positively affect many pathologies. They contain many amino acids that keep anxiety under control and reduce stress, helping us to overcome problems like insomnia or tachycardia. Plus, more good news for us, pumpkins are "biologically correct": they can grow in qualitatively poor terrain, without the help of chemical fertilizers.

Dessert is Served

From appetizers to desert, including bread, pies, focaccia, pizza and breadsticks, the pumpkin is truly a shape shifter. It is vegetable, yes, but its pulp is as sweet as a fruit. A special sweet that can be increased without using too much sugar, becoming the main flavor in a long series of original desserts, from puddings to tarts, strudel to cookies. However it can also be deliciously accompanied by stronger ingredients, such as rich cheeses, sausage, mushrooms or truffles.

Pumpkins morph into creams, soups, gratin, but also into ice cream, frappes and jams. They can be baked, steamed or boiled, sautéed or fried. Is there anything this magical vegetable can't do?

And what about pumpkin seeds? Other than being a veritable concentration of precious nutritive substances – like phytosterols, healthy fats and omega-3 – and having beneficial properties, once toasted and lightly salted they are the perfect snack, both alone or added to a soup, pasta or a vegetable side-dish. If you want to toast them, in order to preserve their qualities, you should roast them at low heat for about 30 minutes, or until they become amber, rather than at a high temperature for a short time. You can also eat them raw.

This vegetable can also become a practical container. Emptied of its pulp and cut so that you get a lid and a little hole for the ladle, it can be used as a soup pot for risotto or pumpkin minestrone, as a salad bowl for pumpkin salad, or even a bowl to serve an appetizing pumpkin curry in...

In the end, there are a limitless amount of uses for this humble vegetable!

Secrets for Choosing and Conserving

Pumpkins should be selected based on the recipe that you intend to make. The "Bologna Grey", for example, is excellent for preparing jams, while the variety called "Priest's Hat", typical in the lowlands of Reggio Emilia and Mantua, is ideal for stuffed pastas. When you buy a whole pumpkin, it is important to check that the vegetable is fresh, hard and ripe: the stalk must be soft and well attached, the rind shouldn't have dents in it. If you gently knock on its surface, you should hear a dull thud. If the pumpkin is purchased in pieces or slices, you should still check to see if it is fresh, ripe and hard, that the cut piece isn't dry and that the seeds are still wet and slippery.

A whole pumpkin can be conserved in a dark, fresh and dry environment, with a temperature between 64°F and 71°F (18°C and 22°C) - just like at home - for many months (although, in keeping with tradition, should be eaten before Carnival). If it is already sliced, it should be kept in the refrigerator in the crisper and wrapped in cellophane so it doesn't dry out; it should be consumed fairly quickly, within a few days, because it tends to dehydrate.

The pulp can be conserved in freezer bags: it's best to cut it into cubes and boil a few minutes before putting it in. If you do freeze it raw, you should clean it, removing the rind, seeds and filaments, and then put it into freezer bags. When you cook it, you need to use it frozen because if it thaws it could lose all its water and become unusable.

Typical and Atypical Recipes

In the Po Valley region, pumpkins have always been loved. They provide the unmistakable flavor of the stuffing of those little trunks of fresh pasta that are the famous Mantua Tortelli, the traditional first-course served on Christmas Eve, and Ferrara Cappellacci, already included in the renaissance cookbooks of the Dukes of Este, where they were recommended for hosting princes, diplomats and illustrious guests.

Originally a poor ingredient in farmers' kitchens, over time pumpkins rose to honor nobility and their courts, becoming more precious and enriched with new flavors to finally conquer tables all over the peninsula.

Our magical vegetable has also always had a close friendship with rice, like in the traditional pumpkin risotto served in the entire Lombard-Veneto area, and welcomed pasta with open arms, like the classic Milanese pumpkin minestrone.

Academia Barilla, an international center dedicated to sharing Italian gastronomic culture, has selected 50 pumpkin recipes for this book.

Some are traditional Italian dishes, like pumpkin gnocchi, while others are born from the Italians' typical creative intelligence that unites excellent products from various regions, paying close attention to the quality of the raw materials, the subtle balance between tradition and innovation and the lively spirit of the final result, that can also take a brief detour into other culinary universes.

12

APPETIZERS
AND SNACKS

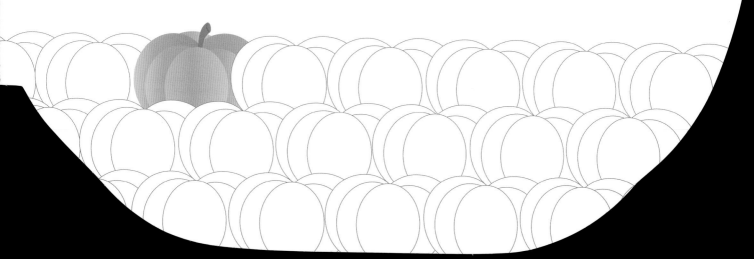

PUMPKIN
SEED STICKS

INGREDIENTS FOR **4** PEOPLE

7 oz. (200 g) puff pastry
7/8 oz. (25 g) shelled pumpkin seeds
1 egg
1 pinch of salt

PREPARATION

Roll the pastry down to 1/12 inch (2 millimeters) thickness,
brush with a little water and sprinkle pumpkin seeds over half.
Fold the part without seed over the other and lightly
press the whole thing to stick the two sides together.
Cut little diamond shapes, about 1 inch (2 1/2 centimeters) wide, and twist them.
Then put them in rows on a baking tray lined with baking paper.
Brush them with beaten egg and dust with a pinch of salt.
Bake at 390°F (200°C) for about 25 minutes.

Preparation time: 20' Cooking time: 25'
Difficulty: easy

PUMPKIN
CREAM PUFFS

INGREDIENTS FOR **4** PEOPLE

For the cream puffs
1/4 cup (50 ml) water
7/8 oz. (25 g) butter
4 tbsp. (30 g) flour
1 egg
1 pinch of salt

For the filling
5 oz. (150 g) pumpkin
1 cup (250 ml) milk
2 oz. (60 g) spicy provolone
3/4 oz. (20 g) butter
2 1/2 tbsp. (20 g) flour
salt and pepper

PREPARATION

For the cream puffs, combine the water, butter in pieces and a pinch of salt in a small pot.
Boil and add all of the sifted flour. Mix with a wooden spoon until it doesn't stick to the pot.
Pour it into a bowl and let it cool and add the egg.
Put it into a pastry bag with a smooth, 1/2 inch (1 centimeter) mouth and form puffs as big as a nut
on a buttered baking pan. Bake at 390°F (200°C) for about 20 minutes, opening the oven during
the last 5 minutes to dry them well. In the meanwhile, shell the pumpkin, removing the seeds, and cut it
into 1/12-1/8 inch (2-3 millimeters) cubes. Melt the butter in a pan, add the pumpkin and brown
on low heat for 3-4 minutes. Add salt, pepper and the flour. Cook for another minute, then add the milk.
Continue mixing, cooking it until it boils for 1 minute. Remove from the heat,
letting it cool slightly and add the provolone cut into cubes as big as the pieces of pumpkin.
Cut open the top of the puff without completely removing it and fill with the pumpkin cream.
If necessary, warm in the over for a few minutes.

Preparation time: 35' Cooking time: 25'
Difficulty: medium

PUMPKIN BLINIS

INGREDIENTS FOR **4** PEOPLE

4 eggs
7 oz. (200 g) pumpkin
1/2 cup (50 g) flour
1 tbsp. plus 2 tsp. (25 ml) extra virgin olive oil
1 bunch of chives,
parsley, mint and chervil
salt and black pepper

PREPARATION

Wash the pumpkin, cut it into pieces and bake at 350°F (180°C)
for about 30 minutes or until it is soft.
If it browns too much, cover with aluminum foil.
Let cool, removing seeds and filaments, then blend and measure out 3 1/2 oz. (100 grams).
Clean and dry the aromatic herbs, then chop them.
Beat the egg in a bowl with the herbs, flour, pumpkin purée salt and pepper.
Warm a pan for the blinis with a bit of oil and spoon
in the mixture in 4 separate parts.
As soon as they are solid, flip them and finish cooking.

Preparation time: 40' Cooking time: 5'
Difficulty: easy

SCALLOPS
WITH PUMPKIN CITRUS

INGREDIENTS FOR **4** PEOPLE

1 lb. 10 oz. (750 g) pumpkin
12 scallops
2 tbsp. (30 ml) extra virgin olive oil
2 oranges

2 grapefruit
2 pink grapefruits
chives
salt and pepper

PREPARATION

Wash the pumpkin, cut it into pieces and bake at 350°F (180°C) for about 30 minutes
or until it is soft. If it browns too much, cover with aluminum foil.
Let it cool, removing seeds and filaments, then blend it with salt,
pepper and a little oil to obtain a dense purée.
Peel the citrus fruits, separating the wedges and eliminating the skin,
and keep the juice obtained during this process.
Clean the scallops, dry them and salt and pepper.
Brown the scallops for a few minutes in an nonstick pan with a little extra virgin olive oil or on a grill.
Slightly warm the citrus fruit on a baking tray with their juice.
With a pastry bag, distribute a dab of pumpkin purée in the center of each shell.
Then put one scallop on each shell, resting it on the purée,
lining it with the citrus wedges and sprinkling them with juice.
Garnish with a few drops of extra virgin olive oil and a finely minced chives,
decorating each shell with a blade of it.

Preparation time: 30' Cooking time: 35'
Difficulty: medium

SAVORY
PUMPKIN CROISSANTS

INGREDIENTS FOR **4** PEOPLE

For the dough
4 cups (500 g) flour "00"
1 cup (250 ml) water
1 egg
1 1/2 tbsp. (20 g) sugar
3 1/2 tbsp. (20 g) yeast

1 tbsp. plus 2 tsp. (25 g) butter
2 tsp. (12 g) salt

For the filling
3 1/2 oz. (100 g) chopped cooked
pumpkin (double that amount
of raw pumpkin)

2 tbsp. plus 1 tsp. (15 g) grated
Parmigiano Reggiano
salt and pepper

For the garnish
1 egg
poppy seeds

PREPARATION

Put the flour in a mound on the pastry board, break the egg in the middle and add the sugar.
Add water little by little with the yeast dissolved in it. Add softened butter and then salt.
Work the dough until it is smooth and elastic. Let it rise, covered by a plastic bowl
in a warm and dry place for 30 minutes. Meanwhile, wash the pumpkin, cut into pieces and bake
at 350°F (180°C) for about 30 minutes or until it is soft. If it browns too much, cover with aluminum foil.
Let it cool, eliminating seeds and filaments, blend it and weigh out 3 1/2 oz. (100 grams).
Combine with grated Parmigiano Reggiano and spice with salt and pepper.
On the pastry board, roll out the dough to 1/8 inch (3 millimeters) and cut into isosceles triangles.
Put a dab of pumpkin filling on the short side and roll it into croissants.
Arrange them on a baking pan covered in baking paper. Let them rise until they double in size
(about 1 hour), then brush them with beaten egg and dust them with poppy seeds.
Bake at 390°-425°F (200°-220°C) for about 20 minutes.

Preparation time: 1 h Rising time: 1 h 30'
Cooking time: 20' Difficulty: medium

PUMPKIN CREAM
WITH CHEESE MOUSSE

INGREDIENTS FOR **4** PEOPLE

1 lb (500 g) pumpkin
1 cup (200 g) whipping cream
9 oz. (250 g) fresh goat cheese
thyme, marjoram and rosemary
salt and pepper

PREPARATION

Clean the pumpkin, removing the rind, seeds and filaments,
then weigh out 10 1/2 oz. (300 grams). Cut into pieces and put into a casserole,
cover with water and boil.
When done, strain the extra water and blend the pumpkin.
Salt and pepper. When the pumpkin cools, add the whipped cream.
To prepare the cheese mousse, stir the goat cheese until creamy
and add the chopped aromatic herbs.
Put pumpkin cream into individual bowls and, on top,
doll up of goat cheese mousse, then serve.

Preparation time: 20' Cooking time: 45'
Difficulty: easy

FRIED STUFFED
PUMPKIN BLOSSOMS

INGREDIENTS FOR 4 PEOPLE

12 pumpkin blossoms

For the filling
10 1/2 oz. (300 g) ricotta
2/3 cup (60 g) grated Parmigiano Reggiano
1 tbsp chopped parsley
1 sprig of marjoram peeled
salt and pepper

For the batter
3 tbsp. plus 1 tsp. (50 ml) milk
1/2 cup (70 g) flour "0"
2 eggs
2 egg yolks
olive oil for frying
salt

PREPARATION

Clean the pumpkin blossoms and remove the pistil, making sure not to break the membranes.
With a wooden spoon, mix the ingredients listed to make the filling, then add the salt and pepper.
With a pastry bag, fill each blossom.
In a mixing bowl, briskly mix the ingredients for the batter.
Lightly flour the blossoms and dip into the batter, then fry a few at a time.
Once drained of excess oil, arrange them on paper towels, salt and serve immediately.

Preparation time: 30' Cooking time: 5-6'
Difficulty: medium

PUMPKIN
AND LEEK FLAN

INGREDIENTS FOR 4-6 PEOPLE

1 lb. 2 oz. (500 g) pumpkin
1/2 cup (100 ml) fresh cream
10 1/2 oz. (300 g) leeks
1/2 cup (50 g) grated Parmigiano Reggiano
2 eggs

1/2 cup (100 ml) milk
1 oz. (30 g) butter
salt and pepper
flour
oil for frying

PREPARATION

Wash the pumpkin, cut into pieces and bake at 350°F (180°C)
for about 30 minutes or until it is soft. If it browns too much, cover with aluminum foil.
Let it cool, eliminating seeds and filaments, blend it and measure out 10 1/2 oz. (300 grams).
Clean the leeks, jetting the green part. Finely slice half and simmer them with half
of the butter on low heat in a frying pan, then salt and pepper.
Once cooked, blend them with the cream, pumpkin, egg and grated Parmigiano Reggiano.
Blend again and, if necessary, add salt.
Cut the remaining leeks into strips and soak them in milk.
Butter the individual molds and fill them with the pumpkin mix.
Bake in a double boiler at 300°F (150°C) for about 40 minutes. In the meantime,
drain the leek strips, flour and fry without changing their color.
Drain on paper towels. Then the flan is done, remove from oven
and wait a few minutes for them to cool. Then flatten them and garnish with the fried leeks.

Preparation time: 30' Cooking time: 40'
Difficulty: easy

28

PUMPKIN FRITTELLE

INGREDIENTS FOR 4 PEOPLE

14 oz. (400 g) pumpkin
1/2 cup (100 ml) water
1 3/4 oz. (50 g) butter
1/2 cup (60 g) flour
2 eggs

1/3 cup (30 g) grated
Parmigiano Reggiano
nutmeg
oil for frying
salt

PREPARATION

Wash the pumpkin, cut into pieces and bake at 350°F (180°C) for about 30 minutes or until it is soft.
If it browns too much, cover with aluminum foil. Let it cool, eliminating seeds and filaments,
blend it and weigh out 7 oz. (200 grams). Combine with grated Parmigiano Reggiano
and a pinch of nutmeg. In the meantime, put the water
and diced butter into a pot with a pinch of salt. Boil and put all the previously sifted flour,
mixing well with a wooden spatula until it doesn't stick to the sides.
Remove from heat and let cool, then add the eggs, one at a time.
Combine the two mixtures and add salt, if necessary.
Heat the oil in a pan and fry the fritelle,
delicately dropping them into the oil using a spoon.
Drain and dry on paper towels.

Preparation time: 50' Cooking time: 5'
Difficulty: medium

PUMPKIN SWEETBREAD

INGREDIENTS FOR **4-6** PEOPLE

2 1/4 cups (280 g) wheat flour
water
7 oz. (200 g) baked pumpkin
(double that amount of raw pumpkin)

3 tbsp. (40 g) sugar
4 1/4 tsp. (20 g) butter
2 tbsp. (12 g) yeast
1 pinch of salt

PREPARAZIONE

Mix 1/2 cup (70 grams) of flour with 50 milliliters of water and yeast in a bowl.
Cover with plastic wrap and let rise in a warm place until it doubles in volume (about 1 hour).
Meanwhile, wash the pumpkin, cut into pieces and bake at 350°F (180°C) for about 30 minutes
or until it is soft. If it browns too much, cover with aluminum foil. Let it cool,
eliminating seeds and filaments, blend it and measure out 7 oz. (200 grams).
When the dough is ready, put the rest of the flour onto a pastry board and put the pumpkin pulp and
sugar in the middle and add the risen dough ball. Start to knead with water to get soft but homogenous
dough (the amount of water depends on the pumpkin's humidity), adding salt as necessary.
When the dough starts to become homogeneous, add room temperature softened butter and the
previous dough. Knead until obtaining homogenous and elastic dough.
Let rest at room temperature, covered with a plastic bowl for about 20 minutes.
Then form little balls. Arrange them in a buttered plumb cake form and let rise,
covered with a bowl, for 1 hour or until the dough comes over the edges.
Bake at 350°F (180°C) for about 25 minutes.

Preparation time: 1 h Rising time: 2 h 20'
Cooking time: 25' Difficulty: medium

PUMPKIN
BREAD

INGREDIENTS FOR **4-6** PEOPLE

4 cups (500 g) wheat flour
1 cup (225 ml) water
5 1/4 oz. (150 g) baked pumpkin
(double that amount of raw pumpkin)

1 1/2 tbsp. (20 ml)
extra virgin olive oil
2 tbsp. (12 g) yeast
2 tsp. (13 g) salt

PREPARATION

Shell the pumpkin and cut into 1 3/4 oz. (50 grams) pieces.
Wrap in aluminum foil and bake for 20 minutes.
Once cooked, let cool.
Put the flour on a pastry board and knead with room temperature water with the yeast dissolved in it.
Slowly add the oil, some salt and the pumpkin.
Continue kneading until obtaining soft, homogeneous and elastic dough.
Let the dough rest, covered with a plastic bowl, for about 10 minutes and then shape into long strands.
Arrange the strands, spaced apart, on a baking tray covered in baking paper
and let rise for 1 hour, covered with plastic.
Bake at 350°F (180°C) for about 18-25 minutes, depending on size.

Preparation time: 1 h Rising time: 1 h 10'
Cooking time: 18-25' Difficulty: medium

PIZZA WITH PUMPKIN
AND SPICY PROVOLONE

INGREDIENTS FOR 4 PEOPLE

For the dough
5 cups (650 g) flour for pizza
1 1/2 cups (375 ml) water
1 1/2 tsp. (5 g) yeast
1 tbsp. (18 g) salt

For the garnish
7 oz. (200 g) Provolone cheese
2 lbs. 3 oz. (1 kg) pumpkin
extra virgin olive oil
rosemary
salt

PREPARATION

On a pastry board, mix the flour with water and yeast, adding salt dissolved in water last.
Let rise, covered by a plastic bowl in a warm place until double the volume
(from 1 to 4 hours, depending on the temperature).
Divide the dough into 4 parts and roll into balls. Let rise, again covered with a plastic bowl,
until they double in size (from 30 minutes to 1 hour 30 minutes, depending on the temperature).
Shell the pumpkin, removing the seeds, cut it into large slices and bake at 350°F (180°C)
for about 25 minutes. Blend with a pinch of salt and a tablespoon of oil;
if the mixture is too dense, add a few drops of water. Thinly slice the provolone.
Abundantly flour the pastry board and flatten the dough balls, starting
with the ends of your fingers and continuing with a revolving movement with your hands.
Spread the pumpkin on the pizzas and add the cheese.
Put the pizzas in the oven and cook at 480°F (250°C) for about 8 minutes.
Once removed from oven, season with a few rosemary leaves and olive oil.

Preparation time: 30' Rising time: 1 h 30' – 5 h 30'
Cooking time: 8' Difficulty: medium

SAVORY
PUMPKIN PIE

INGREDIENTS FOR **4** PEOPLE

10 1/2 oz. (300 g) puff pastry
1 lb. 11 oz. (750 g) pumpkin
1/2 cup (125 ml) cream
2 eggs
3/4 cup (80 g) grated Parmigiano Reggiano
nutmeg
salt and pepper

PREPARATION

Wash the pumpkin, cut into pieces and bake at 350°F (180°C) for 30 minutes or until it is soft.
If it browns too much, cover with aluminum foil. Let it cool, eliminating seeds and filaments,
and blend it. Pour it into a bowl and add the egg, the grated Parmigiano Reggiano and cream.
Flavor with salt, pepper and a little grated nutmeg.
Roll out the pastry to 1/8 inch (3 millimeters) thick and put into a pie mold.
Pour in the pumpkin mix and smooth the surface.
Bake at 350°F (180°C) for 30 minutes.

Preparation time: 60' Cooking time: 30'
Difficulty: easy

GOAT CHEESE
AND PUMPKIN PIE

INGREDIENTS FOR **4** PEOPLE

7 oz. (200 g) puff pastry
9 oz. (250 g) pumpkin
3 oz. (80 g) goat cheese
1/3 cup (80 ml) cream
1 egg
salt and pepper

PREPARATION

Wash the pumpkin, cut into pieces and bake at 350°F (180°C) for 30 minutes or until it is soft.
If it browns too much, cover with aluminum foil. Let it cool, eliminating seeds and filaments,
blend it and weigh out 4 1/2 oz. (125 grams). Roll the past ry to 1/12-1/8 inch (2-3 millimeters) thick
and cover 4 individual molds (or a pie dish) with it.
On the side, prepare mixture with the pumpkin, egg and cream.
Flavor with salt and pepper. Pour the pumpkin mix into the molds,
cover with goat cheese and bake at 350°F (180°C) for about 20 minutes
(30 minutes if in a single pie dish).

Preparation time: 50' Cooking time: 20-30'
Difficulty: easy

42

FIRST COURSES

PUMPKIN CREAM
WITH CANNELLINI BEANS

INGREDIENTS FOR **4** PEOPLE

1 lb. 2 oz. (500 g) pumpkin (to clean)
1 lb. 5 oz. (600 g) potatoes
3 1/2 oz. (100 g) onions
7 oz. (200 g) beans
6 cups (1.5 l) water

2 tsp. (10 ml) extra virgin olive oil
1 sprig of thyme
1 sprig of rosemary
salt and pepper

PREPARATION

Peel the pumpkin and peel the potatoes, then cut them into small pieces.
Clean and slice the onion.
Place these ingredients in a saucepan, cover with water and boil.
Once boiled, blend the vegetables with their cooking broth.
If necessary, dilute the cream with some water, then add salt and pepper.
On the side, boil the beans after they have been soaked for 12 hours in about 8 cups (2 liters) of water.
Just before serving, stir in the beans to the cream.
Top with chopped thyme and rosemary, ground pepper and a drizzle of olive oil.

Preparation time: 20' Soaking time: 12 h
Cooking time: 45' Difficulty: easy

BUCKWHEAT CREPES WITH PUMPKIN AND CHIODINI MUSHROOMS

INGREDIENTS FOR **4-6** PEOPLE

For the crepes
(for 16 crepes, 9 inches /
22 cm in diameter)
2 1/2 cups (330 g)
buckwheat flour
3 cups (750 ml) water
2 tsp. (10 ml)
extra virgin olive oil
1 egg

3 tsp. (15 g) salt
1/3 oz. (10 g) butter, melted

For the filling
2 lbs. 5oz. (1 kg) pumpkin
9 oz. (250 g) chiodini
mushrooms
5 tsp. (25 ml)
extra virgin olive oil

3 oz. (80 g) smoked
scamorza cheese
2 cloves of garlic
1 tbsp chopped
parsley
a few sprigs of thyme

For the sauce
1/3 oz. (10 g) butter, melted

PREPARATION

Mix the ingredients of the crepes batter in a blender and let the mixture rest in the refrigerator for at east an hour. Clean the mushrooms and wash the pumpkin, removing skin and seeds and cut 14 oz. (400 grams) into cubes. Bake or steam the rest and blend it.
Heat the oil in a pan and flavor with peeled garlic and a few sprigs of thyme, removing them after a couple of minutes. Add the pumpkin cubes and after about two minutes, then the mushrooms. Add salt and pepper. Cook, keeping the vegetables crispy, then sprinkle with parsley. Allow to cool and add 7 oz. (200 grams) of pumpkin and smoked cheese cubes. Prepare the crepes (ingredients are for 16 crepes, 9 inches (22 centimeters) in diameter, for 4-6 people they serve eight, you can freeze the rest). Put the pumpkin stuffing on top. Fold them closed as you please (in half, in thirds...) and arrange on a buttered casserole dish. Sprinkle with a little melted butter and bake at 180 ° C for 7-8 minutes.

Preparation time: 50' Resting time: 1 h
Cooking time: 7-8' Difficulty: medium

PUMPKIN GNOCCHI
WITH SAUSAGE AND SAFFRON

INGREDIENTS FOR **4** PEOPLE

For the gnocchi
14 oz. (400 g) pumpkin,
flesh already cooked
(double that
amount of raw pumpkin)
3 1/2 oz. (100 g) freshly
grated bread
1 cup (100 g) flour
1 egg

1 tbsp (6 g) grated
Parmigiano Reggiano
Nutmeg
Salt (fine and coarse)
and pepper

For the sauce
7 oz. (200 g) sausage
10 1/2 oz. (300 g) leeks

4 tbsp (50 ml)
extra virgin olive oil
1 tbsp (8 g) flour
0.005 oz. (0.15 g) saffron
1/2 cup (50 g) grated
Parmigiano Reggiano

PREPARATION

Cut the pumpkin, rind included, into 1 1/2-2 inches (3-4 centimeters) thick slices and bake at 350°-375°F (180°-190°C) in a pan, on a layer of coarse salt without anything else. Cook it until very soft.
Blend the pumpkin and mix in a bowl with the flour, bread crumbs, egg and a tablespoon of grated Parmigiano Reggiano. Spice with nutmeg, salt and pepper. After finishing the dough, form long cylinders of 1 inch (2 centimeters) in diameter and cut into pieces 1 inch (2 centimeters) in length to obtain the gnocchi. Finely chop the leek and let it soak with the oil in a pan. Add the sausage crumbled into pieces without the skin. Brown in the pan then sprinkle with the flour and cook for 1 minute, then pour a ladle of hot water and simmer for another 5 minutes. Finally, add the saffron dissolved in a few tablespoons of water. Cook the gnocchi in boiling salted water for a few minutes. Once they rise to the surface, drain and toss in the pan with the sauce, adding Parmigiano Reggiano cheese.

Preparation time: 40' Cooking time: 3-4'
Difficulty: easy

PUMPKIN
AND BEET SOUP

INGREDIENTS FOR **4** PEOPLE

1 lb. (450 g) pumpkin
10 1/2 oz. (300 g) beets
2 oz. (50 g) onion
1 1/2 oz. (40 g) carrot
1 1/2 oz. (40 g) celery
2 tbsp. (25 ml) extra virgin olive oil
salt

PREPARATION

Wash the beets and separate the white part from the green leaf.
Cut the white part into small cubes and the leaves into strips.
Clean the pumpkin removing skin, seeds and filaments and cut into 1/2 inch (1 centimeter) cubes.
Peel the onion, prepare the carrot and celery, then chopped them and sauté
with extra virgin olive oil in a pan.
Add the white beets and diced pumpkin and sauté for a couple of minutes, then add the leaves.
Cover with water, salt lightly, and cook for about half an hour.

Preparation time: 20' Cooking time: 30'
Difficulty: easy

PENNE WITH PUMPKIN, MUSHROOMS AND BALSAMIC VINEGAR

INGREDIENTS FOR 4 PEOPLE

11 oz. (320 g) penne
10 1/2 oz. (300 g) pumpkin
7 oz. (200 g) porcini mushrooms (ceps)
2 oz. (50 g) shallots
2 tbsp. (25 ml) extra virgin olive oil
3 cups (750 ml) of water

1 tbsp. chopped parsley
1 sprig of rosemary
1 clove of garlic
Balsamic Vinegar of Modena
salt and pepper

PREPARATION

Peel the pumpkin, removing the seeds and cut it into 1cm cubes.
Put the pumpkin cubes, with the shallots and a pinch of salt in a saucepan.
Pour about 3 cups (750 milliliters) of water (or enough to cover everything) and boil the vegetables.
Once cooked, blend to obtain a cream. If necessary, add a little cooking water
to obtain a slightly dense cream. Chop the rosemary and peeled garlic.
In a frying pan, heat half the oil on medium heat, then sauté the diced pumpkin with salt and pepper.
Put the pumpkin aside and, in the same pan, sauté the mushrooms with the remaining oil with the garlic,
rosemary and half of the chopped parsley. Continue cooking for about 2 minutes, then add the diced
pumpkin and cream. Boil the pasta in salted boiling water until al dente, drain and add to the pumpkin
sauce, sautéing everything. Serve sprinkled with the remaining chopped parsley
and a few drops of balsamic vinegar of Modena.

Preparation time: 40' Cooking time: 10'
Difficulty: easy

PUMPKIN RAVIOLI

INGREDIENTS FOR 4 PEOPLE

For the dough
2 cups (200 g) white flour
2 eggs

For the filling
1 lb. 2 oz. (500 g) pumpkin
6 oz. (170 g) ricotta
2 oz. (45 g) grated
Parmigiano Reggiano

3/4 oz. (20 g) shallots
2 1/2 oz. (60 g) sausage
2 1/2 oz. (60 g) porcini
mushrooms (ceps)
1 clove garlic
1 tbsp. (15 ml) extra virgin olive oil
thyme
nutmeg

salt and pepper

For the fondue
3 1/2 oz. (100 g) Fontina cheese
1/2 cup (100 ml) milk
1 egg yolk

For the sauce
2 oz. (40 g) butter

PREPARATION

Mix flour and eggs, then let the dough rest for 30 minutes. Clean the pumpkin, keeping 2 oz. (50 grams) aside, and cut the rest into pieces and bake at 350°F (180°C) until soft. Let cool, remove the seeds and filaments and blend everything. Clean the mushrooms and 50 grams of pumpkin and cut into 1/8-1/6 inch (3-4 millimeters) cubes. Heat the oil in a pan with the chopped shallots, thyme and garlic, add the sausage and brown. Add the diced pumpkin and cook for a few minutes. Add the mushrooms, salt and cook for another 2-3 minutes. Mix the ricotta with 4 oz. (120 grams) of cooked pumpkin, Parmigiano Reggiano cheese, salt, pepper and nutmeg. Roll a sheet of dough, spread the filling with a pastry bag forming rings of 4 inches (10 centimeters) in diameter. Put a spoonful of the pumpkin, mushroom and sausage mixture in the center, then cover with another sheet of pasta. Seal the edges and cut the ravioli with pastry rings. Reduce diced Fontina cheese, cover with milk and leave to infuse for 30 minutes. Add the egg and cook over low heat or in a double boiler until obtaining a smooth cream. Cook the ravioli in salted water and serve with melted butter, pumpkin cream and fondue.

Preparation time: 1 h 30' Cooking time: 4'
Difficulty: medium

PUMPKIN RISOTTO
WITH CRISPY BACON

INGREDIENTS FOR 4 PEOPLE

1 lb. 2 oz. (500 g) pumpkin
1 tbsp. (15 ml) extra virgin olive oil
10 1/2 oz. (300 g) Carnaroli rice
1 small onion
1/4 cup (50 ml) dry white wine

6 cups (1.5 l) vegetable broth
3 1/2 oz. (100 g) bacon sliced
2 1/2 oz. (60 g) butter
1 cup (80 g) grated Parmigiano Reggiano
salt

PREPARATION

Dice half of the bacon and place in the oven or in a pan along with the remaining
slices until crisp. Clean the pumpkin, removing the seeds and rind.
Dice 5 1/4 oz. (150 grams) of 1/2 inch (5 millimeters) cubes from the side, leaving the rest in large chunks of
pumpkin. Chop the onion and put a third in a pan with the oil. Let it brown and add the chunks of pumpkin,
cover with broth and cook for about 15 minutes or until the pumpkin starts to fall apart, then blend.
Meanwhile, in another pan, cook the remaining onion with 3/4 oz. (20 grams) of butter,
then add the pumpkin cubes. Add the rice and toast it well.
Add the wine and let it evaporate completely, always stirring.
Continue cooking, adding pumpkin broth gradually, stirring often.
Once cooked, remove from the heat and stir in the remaining butter and Parmigiano Reggiano cheese,
adding the previously prepared pumpkin cream and crispy bacon cubes.
Season with salt and garnish with the remaining cream and slices of bacon.

Preparation time: 40' Cooking time: 16-18'
Difficulty: easy

PUMPKIN TORTELLI

INGREDIENTS FOR 4 PEOPLE

For the pastry
2 1/2 cups (300 g) white flour
3 eggs

For the filling
2 lbs. 4 oz. (1 kg) pumpkin
1 1/2 cups (150 g) grated

Parmigiano Reggiano
2 1/2 oz. (50 g) crushed
macaroons
2 oz. (40 g) Cremona
Mostarda
2 tbsp. breadcrumbs
1 egg

nutmeg
salt

For the dressing
3 oz. (80 g) butter
2 1/2 oz. (60 g) grated
Parmigiano Reggiano

PREPARATION

Place the flour on a pastry board, break the eggs in the center and work until dough is smooth
and homogeneous. Wrap in plastic wrap and let rest for 20 minutes. Cut the pumpkin into thick slices,
removing the seeds and bake at 350°F (180°C) for 25 minutes.
When soft, remove the peel and blend it.
Mix the pumpkin purée, egg, cheese, macaroons, Mostarda, a sprinkle of nutmeg and a pinch of salt.
If it's not solid, add one or two tablespoons of breadcrumbs.
With a rolling pin, roll out the dough to a thickness of 1 mm. Using a pastry bag put a teaspoon
of pumpkin on the sheet of dough, appropriately spaced apart about 8 inches (20 centimeters).
When finished, lay another sheet of pasta on top and, with the notched wheel,
cut the ravioli into squares, each measuring about 6 inches (15 centimeters) on each side.
Seal the edges well to prevent the filling from spilling out. Cook the ravioli in salted water, drain with
a slotted spoon, then toss them in a pan with butter and Parmigiano Reggiano cheese.

Preparation time: 45' Resting time: 20'
Cooking time: 3-4' Difficulty: medium

PUMPKIN, CHESTNUT AND MILK SOUP

INGREDIENTS FOR 4 PEOPLE

1 lb. 2 oz. (500 g) pumpkin
5 cups (1 l) milk
9 oz. (250 g) chestnuts
1 sprig of fennel
2 tsp. (10 ml) extra virgin olive oil
4 slices of bread
salt and pepper

PREPARATION

Peel the chestnuts and boil in lightly salted water
with a sprig of fennel for about 15 minutes, then drain.
Meanwhile, cut the bread into cubes and toast in the oven for a few minutes.
Clean the pumpkin, removing skin, seeds and filaments, and cut into large squares.
Put it into a pan with the chestnuts, milk and a pinch of salt.
Bring to a boil, then reduce the heat and simmer until the pumpkin starts to come apart.
At this point, blend everything (you can keep a few chestnuts whole as a garnish).
Serve and season with freshly ground pepper and a drizzle of olive oil.
Serve with croutons.

Preparation time: 45' Cooking time: 30'
Difficulty: easy

62

MAIN COURSES

CODFISH WITH PUMPKIN

INGREDIENTS FOR **4** PEOPLE

12 oz. (350 g) cod fillets soaked
9 oz. (250 g) pumpkin
1 cup (250 ml) milk
4 tbsp. (50 ml) extra virgin olive oil
2 oz. (50 g) onion
thyme
1 clove of garlic
salt and pepper

PREPARATION

Clean the pumpkin and cut into cubes. Fry in a pan with half the olive oil,
the sliced onion, a clove of garlic and a few sprigs of thyme.
Add the salted cod, cut into pieces, and cover with milk, salt and pepper and cook for 5 minutes.
Drain any excess milk, remove the garlic and thyme, then stir in the remaining olive oil.

Preparation time: 20' Cooking time: 30'
Difficulty: easy

STEWED VEAL
WITH PUMPKIN

INGREDIENTS FOR **4** PEOPLE

1 lb. 9 oz. (700 g) veal cut into chunks
2 oz. (50 g) onion
2 oz. (50 g) celery
2 tbsp. plus 1 tsp. (30 ml) extra virgin olive oil
1/2 cup (100 ml) white wine

2 cups (1 l) broth (vegetable or meat)
14 oz. (400 g) pumpkin
7 oz. (200 g) potatoes
thyme, sage and marjoram
salt and pepper

PREPARATION

Peel the pumpkin, removing the seeds and filaments and cut into sticks,
setting aside 2 oz. (50 grams) that to chop.
Peel the onion and celery, chop and brown in a pan with oil,
pumpkin and chopped herbs washed, dried and peeled.
Add the diced veal and fry everything.
Add salt and pepper, then sprinkle with white wine.
Let the wine evaporate and gradually add the broth. Cook for about an hour.
Meanwhile, peel the potatoes, wash and cut into pieces and boil for 5 minutes in salted water,
drain and add to the meat pieces.
Add in the pumpkin sticks and cook for another 15-20 minutes.

Preparation time: 30' Cooking time: 1 h 20'
Difficulty: medium

PUMPKIN
AND SEITAN VEGGIE BURGER

INGREDIENTS FOR 4 PEOPLE

10 1/2 oz. (300 g) pumpkin
4 oz. (120 g) Provolone
12 oz. (350 g) seitan
2 tbsp. (25 ml) extra virgin olive oil
salt and pepper

PREPARATION

Clean the pumpkin, removing the skin, seeds and filaments,
and cut into 1/8-1-6 inch (2-3 millimeters) thick, round slices.
Cut the seitan into four slices.
Cook the slices of pumpkin on a hot grill or a griddle greased with olive oil for a few minutes.
At the same time grill the seitan. Season with salt and pepper.
Meanwhile, slice the provolone into thin slices.
Top the pumpkin patties with seitan and cheese.

Preparation time: 30' Cooking time: 5'
Difficulty: easy

PUMPKIN CURRY

INGREDIENTS FOR **4** PEOPLE

1 lb. 5 oz. (600 g) pumpkin
1 tbsp. (15 ml) extra virgin olive oil
3 1/2 oz. (100 g) onion
2 tbsp. curry powder (or 50 g curry paste)
2 1/2 cups (500 ml) milk (or coconut milk)
salt

PREPARATION

Wash the pumpkin, peel, remove seeds and filaments and cut into cubes of 1/2-1 inch (1-2 centimeters).
Peel the onion and cut into slices. Sauté in a pan with the oil, then add the curry.
Dilute with milk.
Bring to a boil, then add the diced pumpkin and salt.
Simmer for about 20 minutes or until the pumpkin is soft and the sauce thick enough.

Preparation time: 15' Cooking time: 20'
Difficulty: easy

BAKED FRITTATA
WITH PUMPKIN AND ROSEMARY

INGREDIENTS FOR **4** PEOPLE

8 eggs
14 oz. (400 g) pumpkin
1/2 cup (50 g) grated Parmigiano Reggiano
1 tbsp. (15 ml) extra virgin olive oil
1 sprig of rosemary
salt and pepper

PREPARATION

Wash the pumpkin, peel and cut it into pieces, removing seeds and filaments,
then steam for about 20 minutes, or until it is soft but not crumblling
(alternatively, use a pressure cooker for 2-4 minutes).
Cut into cubes about 2 inches (5 centimeters) to the side.
Beat the eggs in a bowl with the grated Parmigiano Reggiano,
salt, pepper and chopped rosemary, then add the diced pumpkin.
Pour into an oiled oven and bake in at 300°F (150°C) for about 20 minutes.

Preparation time: 35' Cooking time: 20'
Difficulty: easy

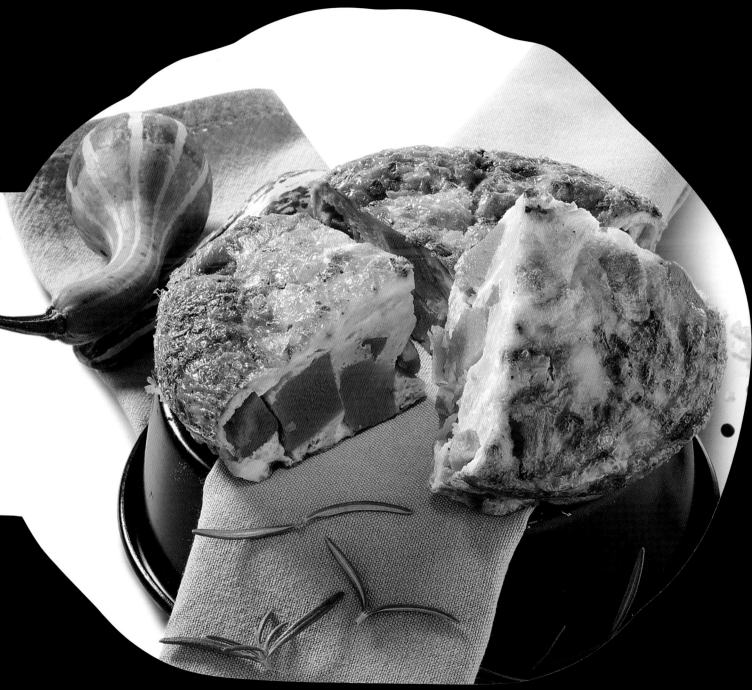

PUMPKIN-STUFFED MUSHROOMS

INGREDIENTS FOR 4 PEOPLE

10 1/2 oz. (300 g) pumpkin
1/2 oz. (12 g) porcini mushrooms (ceps)
1/2 cup (50 g) grated Parmigiano Reggiano
2 tbsp. (25 ml) extra virgin olive oil
2 oz. (50 g) shallot

1/2 clove of garlic
1 tbsp. chopped parsley
1 sprig of rosemary
1 sprig of thyme
salt and pepper

PREPARATION

Peel the pumpkin, removing the seeds and of the filaments and reduce it
into cubes of about 1/8 inch (2 millimeters) thick.
Clean mushrooms and separate stems from the heads. Cut the stems into cubes.
Wash and dry the herbs, then chop the garlic separately from the shallot, rosemary and thyme.
Heat half the oil in a skillet over medium heat, then sauté the diced pumpkin with salt and pepper.
Put aside the pumpkin and, in the same pan, sauté the mushroom stems with the remaining oil with
herbs, the shallot, garlic and half the parsley.
Cook for about 2 minutes, then add the cooked diced pumpkin.
Let cool and add grated Parmigiano Reggiano cheese (keep aside a spoonful) and the remaining parsley,
then check for salt and pepper.
Stuff the mushroom heads, sprinkle with the remaining Parmigiano Reggiano cheese
and bake at 350°F (180°C) for 10 minutes.

Preparation time: 30' Cooking time: 10'
Difficulty: easy

VEAL
AND PUMPKIN ROLLS

INGREDIENTS FOR 4 PEOPLE

12 slices veal (about 14 oz. / 400 g)
14 oz. (400 g) pumpkin
1 oz. (30 g) butter
1 1/4 cups (250 ml) milk
salt and pepper

PREPARATION

Clean the pumpkin and slice thinly.
Put the remnant cuttings (with the exception of the rind) in a pan with a pinch of salt.
Cover with water, bring to a boil and cook until the pumpkin starts to crumble,
then blend in order to obtain a cream.
Beat the veal slices with a meat tenderizer, cover with the pumpkin,
salt and pepper lightly, then roll up.
Close the rolls with one or more toothpicks.
Fry the rolls in the pan with the butter, pour in the milk and, when it boils,
add the pumpkin cream obtained from cuttings.
Season with salt and pepper, and cook for about 15 minutes.

Preparation time: 30' Cooking time: 15'
Difficulty: easy

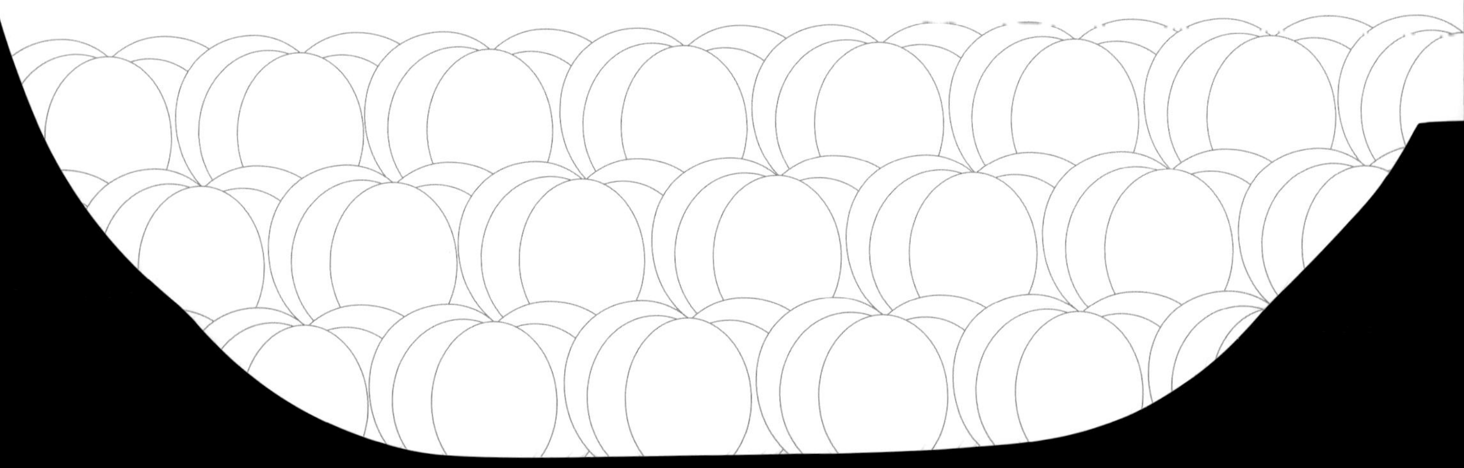

SIDE DISHES

PUMPKIN AND POTATO CROQUETTES

INGREDIENTS FOR **4** PEOPLE

14 oz. (400 g) pumpkin
14 oz. (400 g) potatoes
1/2 cup (50 g) grated
Parmigiano Reggiano
2 eggs

flour for dusting
3 1/2oz. (100 g) breadcrumbs
frying oil
nutmeg
salt

PREPARATION

Wash the pumpkin, peel and cut it into pieces, removing seeds and filaments, then steam with
for about 30 minutes or until soft (alternatively, use a pressure cooker for 3-5 minutes), then blend.
Boil the potatoes in lightly salted boiling water for about 20 minutes.
Once cooked, mash with a potato masher.
Combine the two mixtures, add the Parmigiano Reggiano cheese and two egg yolks.
Season with salt and nutmeg.
Form cylinders and roll in the flour, beaten egg whites and breadcrumbs.
Fry the croquettes in hot oil, drain and dry on paper towels.

Preparation time: 50' Cooking time: 5'
Difficulty: easy

PUMPKIN GRATIN

INGREDIENTS FOR **4** PEOPLE

1 lb. 11 oz. (750 g) pumpkin
3/4 cup (150 ml) fresh cream
1 cup (200 ml) milk
1/2 oz. (10 g) butter for greasing the pan
salt and white pepper

PREPARATION

Peel the pumpkin and remove seeds and filaments,
then cut it into thin slices with the help of a mandolin or slicer.
Pour the cream into a saucepan and add the milk, pumpkin, salt and white pepper.
Cover and cook over moderate heat until the pumpkin is tender.
Grease a baking dish and arrange the slices of pumpkin in layers on it.
Bake at 350°F (180°C) for about 20 minutes, until the surface has colored.
Cool the cake (to get a regular cut) and cut into shapes as desired.
Before serving, warm in the oven at 350°F (180°C) for a few minutes.

Preparation time: 40' Cooking time: 20'
Difficulty: easy

PUMPKIN SALAD
WITH BALSAMIC VINEGAR

INGREDIENTS FOR **4** PEOPLE

12 oz. (350 g) chopped cooked pumpkin
(double that amount of raw pumpkin)
3 1/2 oz. (100 g) mixed greens
1 tbsp. (12 ml) balsamic vinegar
3 tbsp. (35 ml) extra virgin olive oil
2 oz. (40 g) roasted hazelnuts
salt

PREPARATION

Wash the pumpkin, peel and cut it into pieces, removing seeds and filaments,
then steam with for about 20 minutes or until soft but not overcooked
(alternatively, use a pressure cooker for 2-4 minutes).
Let cool, then cut into large dice.
Prepare a sauce by dissolving the salt in vinegar and then mixing with the oil.
Arrange the pumpkin squares on the mixed greens, add the chopped hazelnuts
and season with the balsamic reduction.

Preparation time: 30'
Difficulty: easy

PUMPKIN MILLEFEUILLE

INGREDIENTS FOR **4-6** PEOPLE

10 1/2 oz. (300 g) pumpkin
5 oz. (140 g) mozzarella
4 oz. (120 g) scamorza cheese
3 oz. (90 g) cooked ham, sliced thick
2 tbsp. (25 ml) extra virgin olive oil
salt and pepper

PREPARATION

Clean the pumpkin, removing the skin, seeds and filaments, and cut into thick 1/4-1/3 inch
(5-6 millimeters) slices, then cutting them with 4 inch (10 centimeters) round pastry rings.
Cook the pumpkin discs for a few minutes on a hot grill or a griddle greased with olive oil. Season with
salt and pepper. Meanwhile, reduce into thin slices mozzarella and scamorza, then cut these as well as
the sliced ham using the same 4 inch (10 centimeters) pastry rings.
Assemble the millefeuille alternating the different ingredients
Before serving, heat in the oven for 5 minutes.

Preparation time: 30' Cooking time: 5'
Difficulty: easy

PUMPKIN PURÉE

INGREDIENTS FOR **4** PEOPLE

1 lb. 5 oz. (600 g) pumpkin
1 oz. (30 g) butter
3 tbsp. (20 g) grated Parmigiano Reggiano
nutmeg
salt

PREPARATION

Wash the pumpkin, peel and cut it into pieces, removing seeds and filaments,
then steam for about 30 minutes or until very soft
(alternatively, use a pressure cooker for 3-5 minutes).
Blend and put in a large serving bowl.
Add the butter and Parmigiano Reggiano cheese.
Season with salt and a some grated nutmeg, then serve.

Preparation time: 15' Cooking time: 30'
Difficulty: easy

POLENTA AND PUMPKIN FORM WITH FONDUE

INGREDIENTS FOR **4** PEOPLE

For the form
12 oz. (350 g) pumpkin
1 cup (250 ml) water
1 cup (125 g) flour for polenta
oil to grease the molds
salt (fine and coarse)

For the fondue
3 1/2 oz. (100 g) Fontina
1/2 cup (100 ml) milk
1 egg yolk

PREPARATION

Cut Fontina cheese into cubes, cover with the milk and let it soak for at least 30 minutes.
Add the egg and cook over low heat fondue or water bath to obtain a smooth cream.
Cut the pumpkin with the skin into 1 1/2-2 inch (3-4 centimeters) thick slices, then place in a baking dish
on a layer of coarse salt, without other additions. Cook the pumpkin in the oven
at about 350°-375°F (180°-190°C) until very soft (check using a toothpick).
Blend, then weigh out 9 oz. (250 grams) and put into a pot with water and a pinch of salt.
Bring to a boil and pour the polenta flour in.
Cook for at least half an hour, stirring often, then pour the mixture immediately
into one or more oiled molds. Level the surface and let rest for 10 minutes,
then flip the form onto a serving plate. Drizzle with melted cheese and serve immediately.

Preparation time: 15' Resting time: 30' for the fondue, 10' for the form
Cooking time: 30' Difficulty: medium

92

DESSERTS

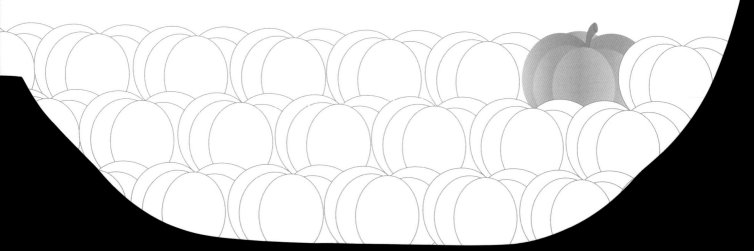

PUMPKIN COOKIES

INGREDIENTS FOR **4** PEOPLE

7 oz. (200 g) pumpkin
10 1/2 oz. (300 g) flour
5 oz. (150 g) brown sugar
3 1/2 oz. (100 g) butter
1 egg

zest of 1/2 lemon
cinnamon
1 pinch salt
cane sugar for decoration

PREPARATION

Wash the pumpkin, peel and cut it into pieces, removing seeds and filaments, then steam for about
30 minutes or until very soft (alternatively, use a pressure cooker for 3-5 minutes),
then blend and weigh out 3 1/2 oz. (100 grams).
Stir the butter with the sugar, add the egg yolk, flour and pumpkin.
Spice with cinnamon and lemon peel to taste and season with a pinch of salt.
Add the flour and knead without overworking the dough, then wrap it in a plastic wrap
and let rest in refrigerator for one hour.
Roll a long 1 1/2 inch (3 centimeters) log on a floured table, brush with egg white and sprinkle
with cane sugar for decoration. Slice the log into discs 1 centimeter thick.
Arrange on a lightly buttered and floured baking sheet (or lined with oven paper)
and bake at 350°-375°F (180°-190°C) for about 20 minutes.

Preparation time: 45' Resting time: 1 h
Cooking time: 20' Difficulty: easy

PUMPKIN DONUTS

INGREDIENTS FOR **4** PEOPLE

2 cups (250 g) flour
4 oz. (125 g) chopped cooked pumpkin
(double that amount of raw pumpkin)
2 tsp. (6 g) yeast
1 tsp. (5 g) sugar
1 oz. (25 g) butter

1 egg
3 tbsp. plus 1 tsp. (50 ml) milk
1 pinch of salt
frying oil
sugar for decoration

PREPARATION

Wash the pumpkin, cut it into pieces and cook in the oven at a temperature of 350°F (180°C) for about half an hour or until soft. If it darkens too much, cover with a sheet of aluminum foil.
Let cool and remove seeds and filaments, then blend and weigh out 4 oz. (125 grams).
Mix the flour with the pumpkin, egg, sugar and yeast dissolved in milk. Mix with the remaining milk.
Last, add room temperature butter and a pinch of salt. Knead until the dough is smooth and elastic.
Cover dough and let it rest for about 30 minutes at room temperature, then roll it out with a rolling pin on floured surface to a thickness of about 1 inch (2 centimeters).
With a cookie-cutter, cut 4 inch (10 centimeters)
discs. Arrange them on a tray covered with a floured towel and let rise until doubled in volume (this will take at least an hour).
Fry the donuts in hot oil until they take on a golden color.
Drain them and put them to dry on paper towels, then sprinkle with sugar.

Preparation time: 40' Rising time: 1 h 30'
Cooking time: 5' Difficulty: medium

PUMPKIN JAM

INGREDIENTS FOR FOUR **12 OZ. (350 ML)** JARS

1 lb. 5 oz. (750 g) chopped cooked pumpkin
(double that amount of raw pumpkin)
1 lb. 4 oz. (700 g) brown sugar
1/3 cup (70 ml) water
juice of 1/2 lemon

PREPARATION

Wash the pumpkin, peel and cut it into pieces, removing seeds and filaments,
then steam for about half an hour or until soft (alternatively, use a pressure cooker for 3-5 minutes).
Allow it to cool, then blend and weigh out 1 lb. 5 oz. (750 grams).
Add the sugar and let it sit for an hour. Then add the water, bring to a boil and add the lemon juice.
Boil for 5 minutes. Pour the jam into the jars heated in the oven,
then seal them turn them upside-down until cooled.

Preparation time: 1 h Resting time: 1 h
Cooking time: 5′ Difficulty: easy

PUMPKIN
CRÈME BRÛLÉE

INGREDIENTS FOR **4** PEOPLE

14 oz. (400 g) pumpkin
3 eggs
2 1/2 oz. (60 g) sugar
1 1/2 cups (300 ml) cream
cinnamon
brown sugar to caramelize

PREPARATION

Wash the pumpkin, peel and cut it into pieces, removing seeds and filaments,
then steam for about 30 minutes or until very soft (alternatively,
use a pressure cooker for 3-5 minutes), then blend and weigh out 7 oz. (200 grams).
In a bowl, beat the eggs with the sugar and a pinch of cinnamon,
add the cream and then the pumpkin and mix.
Pour into baking pans and bake in a water bath at 210°F (100°C) for about 45 minutes.
Let cool and refrigerate for at least an hour before serving.
Sprinkle the cream and a hint of brown sugar and caramelize with a gas torch or under the grill.

Preparation time: 45' Cooking time: 45'
Resting time: 1 h Difficulty: easy

SWEET PUMPKIN CREAM
WITH SPELT AND MACAROONS

INGREDIENTS FOR 4 PEOPLE

1 lb. 2 oz. (500 g) pumpkin
2 1/2 oz. (60 g) spelt
2 tbsp. (25 g) sugar
4 macaroons
milk

PREPARATION

Boil the spelt, after soaking it for about 12 hours.
Clean and cut the pumpkin, put it in a saucepan, cover with water and let it boil.
When cooked, blend with the mixer, sweeten with sugar and dilute the mixture with a little milk.
Last, add the spelt, after having drained it, and pour the cream into individual bowls and let cool.
Before serving, sprinkle with crumbled macaroons.

Preparation time: 20' Soaking time: 12 h
Cooking time: 45' (30' for spelt + 15' for the pumpkin) Difficulty: easy

PUMPKIN
SEED CRISP

INGREDIENTS FOR **4** PEOPLE

7 oz. (200 g) shelled pumpkin seeds
7 oz. (200 g) sugar
2-3 drops of lemon juice
extra virgin olive oil

PREPARATION

Place the pumpkin seeds in a pan and keep warm in the oven about 122°F (50°C).
Put the sugar and lemon juice in a saucepan, preferably copper, not tinned.
Cook everything until it has a golden caramel color, then add the pumpkin seeds warm,
stirring well with a wooden spoon.
Grease with oil a marble top and pour the mixture out.
Hang up to a thickness of an inch or two (a few millimeters),
using a rolling pin also oleate, and before it hardens cut it into strips,
using a large knife, or break it by hand when cold.
Keep the crisp in a tightly closed tin.

Preparation time: 30' Cooking time: 10'
Difficulty: medium

PUMPKIN
AND PINE NUT TART

INGREDIENTS FOR 4 PEOPLE

1 lb. 2 oz. (500 g) pumpkin
9 oz. (250 g) short crust
1 cup (200 ml) cream
1/2 oz. (15 g) cornstarch
2 egg yolks

3 oz. (80 g) sugar
2 1/2 oz. (50 g) pine nuts
2 1/2 oz. (50 g) dessert gelatin
zest of 1/2 lemon
1/2 vanilla pod

PREPARATION

Wash the pumpkin, cut it into pieces and cook in the oven at a temperature of 350°F (180°C) for about half an hour or until soft. If it darkens too much, cover with a sheet of aluminum foil. Let cool and remove seeds and filaments, then blend.
With a whisk, beat the egg yolks with the sugar in a bowl, then add the cornstarch and mix well. Boil the cream in a saucepan with the vanilla pod slit with a small knife, then pour in the beaten egg yolks, stirring well with a whisk and cook as you would a custard. Let the mixture cool down, remove the vanilla, and mix with the pumpkin cream. Flavor with lemon zest. Line a cake tin 8 inches (20 centimeters) in diameter with the pastry, rolled out up to a thickness of 1 1/2 inches (3 millimeters). Fill it with the mixture and level it well. Sprinkle the surface with pine nuts and garnish with strips of pastry obtained from the pastry scraps. If you want, you can brush them with a little beaten egg to get a more golden color. Bake at 350°F (180°C) for about half an hour. Let cool completely before removing the tart, then sprinkle with gelatin.

Preparation time: 45' Cooking time: 25-30'
Difficulty: medium

PUMPKIN FRAPPÉ

INGREDIENTS FOR **4-6** PEOPLE

1 lb. 2 oz. (500 g) pumpkin
3 oz. (75 g) sugar
3/4 cup (150 ml) milk
3 1/2 oz. (100 g) ice cubes
ground cinnamon

PREPARATION

Wash the pumpkin, peel and cut it into pieces, removing seeds and filaments,
then steam for about 30 minutes or until soft
(alternatively, use a pressure cooker for 3-5 minutes),
then blend and weigh out 9 oz. (250 grams).
Allow it to cool, then put the pumpkin in the blender
with the sugar, milk and a pinch of cinnamon.
Add ice and blend.
Pour into glasses and serve.

Preparation time: 40'
Difficulty: easy

ANISEED PUMPKIN JELLY

INGREDIENTS FOR **4** PEOPLE

1 lb. 2 oz. (500 g) pumpkin
1/2 cup (100 ml) water
5 oz. (150 g) brown sugar
1/2 oz. (10 g) agar-agar
aniseed

PREPARATION

Boil the water, add the anise, cover with a sheet of plastic and let for a couple of hours, then filter.
Wash the pumpkin, peel and cut it into pieces, removing seeds and filaments,
then steam for about 30 minutes or until it is very soft
(alternatively, use a pressure cooker for 3-5 minutes), then blend it and weigh out 10 1/2 oz. (300 grams).
In a saucepan, mix the sugar with agar-agar, adding the anise infusion
and boil for one minute, stirring. Then add the pumpkin.
Pour the mixture into a container so as to form a layer of a couple of centimeters.
Let cool completely, then cut to suit.

Preparation time: 45′ Cooking time: 1′
Resting time: 2 h Difficulty: easy

PUMPKIN
ICE CREAM

INGREDIENTS PER APPROX. 2 LBS. 5 OZ. (1 KG) OF ICE CREAM

2 1/2 cups (500 ml) milk
7 oz. (200 g) mashed pumpkin
(double that amount of raw pumpkin)
4 oz. (110 g) sugar
1/3 cup (75 ml) cream

1/2 oz. (20 g) skim milk powder
1/2 oz. (15 g) dextrose
1 tbsp. (15 ml) liquor amaretto
1 tsp. (5 g) stabilizer for ice cream
(or according to manufacturer's instructions)

PREPARATION

Wash the pumpkin, cut it into pieces and bake at 350°F (180°C) for about half an hour or until soft.
If it darkens too much, cover with a sheet of aluminum foil.
Let cool and remove seeds and filaments, then blend it and weigh out 7 oz. (200 grams).
Meanwhile, heat the milk in a saucepan to about 115°-122°F (45°-50°C).
Also, mix the dry sugar, dextrose, milk powder and the stabilizer.
Then slowly pour in warm milk. Bring the mixture to 150°F (65°C),
add the cream and pasteurize at 185°F (85°C). Quickly cool to 40°F (4°C) by putting
the mixture into a container immersed in a basin with water and ice.
Add the baked pumpkin purée, blend well with a blender and allowed to set at 40°F (4°C) for 6 hours.
Then add the liquor and freeze, churning the mixture in an ice cream maker until it is fluffy
and dry in appearance, i.e. not shiny (the time depends on the ice cream maker).

Preparation time: 40' Resting time: 6 h
Difficulty: medium

PUMPKIN AND POPPY PUFFS

INGREDIENTS FOR **4** PEOPLE

7 oz. (200 g) puff pastry

For the filling
12 oz. (350 g) pumpkin
1/2 oz. (20 g) cane sugar
1 tsp. (10 g) honey

1/2 oz (20 g) poppy seeds
1/2 oz. (20 g) butter
1 pinch of salt

For finishing
1 egg

PREPARATION

Wash the pumpkin, peel and remove the seeds, then cut into 1 inch (2 centimeters) pieces.
Coarsely grind the poppy seeds (you can use a coffee grinder) and put them in a pan with the melted butter. Cook over low heat for a few minutes, then add the pumpkin, honey, sugar and a pinch of salt.
Continue cooking until the pumpkin is cook, but still thick. Let cool.
Meanwhile roll the pastry to 2 inches (5 millimeters) thick.
With cookie cutters, cut 4 inch (10 centimeters) discs, roll them with a rolling pin 1-1/2 inch (2-3 millimeters), giving them an oval shape.
Brush the edges with a little beaten egg, place the filling in the center and close the dough up.
Arrange the puff pastry on a baking sheet lined with oven paper, brushing the surface with the remaining beaten egg. Bake at 390°F (200°C) for about 20 minutes.

Preparation time: 40' Cooking time: 20'
Difficulty: easy

STRUDEL WITH PUMPKIN, APPLES, RAISINS AND NUTS

INGREDIENTS FOR **6** PEOPLE

10 1/2 oz. (300 g) puff pastry

For the filling
1 lb. (450 g) apples
10 1/2 oz. (300 g) pumpkin
2 oz. (60 g) walnuts
1 1/2 oz. (40 g) raisins

1 oz. (25 g) butter
3 tbsp. (35 g) cane sugar
zest of 1 lemon

For finishing
1 egg

PREPARATION

Clean the pumpkin, peel and remove the seeds. Cut into slices an inch or two (a few millimeters) thick.
Peel the apples, remove the core and also cut into slices.
Melt the butter in a pan and sauté the pumpkin. After 3-4 minutes, add the apples
and continue cooking for a few minutes, then add the sugar and the lemon zest.
Remove from heat and add the crushed walnuts and raisins soaked for 15 minutes
in warm water and dried. Roll out the puff pastry into a rectangular sheet 1 inch (2 millimeters) thick.
Spread the filling along one side of the dough, brush the edges with a little beaten egg and close.
Arrange the strudel on a baking sheet lined with parchment paper,
making sure that the sealed portion is under the strudel.
After slicing slits on the surface of the cake, brush with the remaining
beaten egg and bake at 340°-350°F (170°-180°C) for about 25 minutes.

Preparation time: 1 h   Cooking time: 25'
Difficulty: medium

CHOCOLATE PUMPKIN CAKE

INGREDIENTS FOR **4-6** PEOPLE

7 oz. (200 g) short crust
14 oz. (400 g) pumpkin
3 1/2 oz. (100 g) flour
6 tbsp. (80 g) sugar
2 oz. (50 g) butter

1 egg
1/2 oz. (16 g) cocoa
1 tsp. (5 g) baking powder
1 pinch of salt

PREPARATION

Wash the pumpkin, peel and cut it into pieces, removing seeds and filaments, then steam for about
10 minutes or until it is not too soft, (alternatively, use a pressure cooker for 2-3 minutes).
Remove about one-third of the pumpkin, letting the rest to cook for another 20 minutes
(alternatively, use a pressure cooker for 3-5 minutes).
Cut the less cooked pumpkin into slices and blend more cooked part.
On a floured surface, roll out the dough with a rolling pin to 1 1/2 inches (3 millimeters).
Line a buttered and floured cake form with the short crust.
Vigorously mix the butter and sugar in a bowl. Add the egg, 3 1/2 oz. (100 grams) of mashed pumpkin,
salt and mix. Stir in the flour with the cocoa and baking powder.
Fill the lined baking pan with the mixture. Arrange the slices of pumpkin
on top of the cake, pressing slightly.
Bake at 340°F (170°C) for about 30 minutes.
Remove from the oven and let cool.

Preparation time: 1 h Cooking time: 30'
Difficulty: medium

PUMPKIN CHEESECAKE

INGREDIENTS FOR **4-6** PEOPLE

For the cream
9 oz. (250 g) chopped cooked pumpkin (double that amount of raw pumpkin)
9 oz. (250 g) ricotta
3/4 cup (150 ml) cream
6 tbsp. (75 g) sugar

1 tsp. (5 g) powdered gelatin

For the jelly
9 oz. (250 g) chopped cooked pumpkin (double that amount of raw pumpkin)
6 tbsp. (75 g) sugar
1 tbsp. (7 g) powdered gelatin

For the crust
2 oz. (50 g) egg white
1 tbsp. (15 g) sugar
1 1/2 oz. (40 g) almonds
3 tbsp. (40 g) powdered sugar

PREPARATION

Wash the pumpkin, peel and cut it into pieces, removing seeds and filaments, and steam until soft, then blend it and weigh out two 9 oz. (250 grams) parts. For the jelly, boil the second part of the pumpkin with sugar and dissolve the gelatin. Let cool. Keep 3-4 spoonfuls apart and pour the rest into a mold smaller than the final cake mold. Freeze. For the crust, finely grind almonds with icing sugar. Aside, whisk the egg whites with the sugar and combine the two mixtures. Form a disc the diameter of the cake on a baking sheet lined with oven paper and bake at 350°F (180°C) for 25 minutes.

For the cream, boil the second part of the pumpkin with sugar, dissolve the gelatin in cold water and dry, let cool. Stir in the cheese and whipped cream. Put the crust into the bottom of a 7-8 inch (18-20 centimeters) mold, add a layer of cream, and then add the jelly). Top with another later of cream and level with a spatula, then freeze. Remove from the mold, garnish with the extra jelly, warmed to make it fluid. Let it the cake thaw completely before serving.

Preparation time: 1 h Freezing: 2 h
Difficulty: high

ALPHABETICAL INDEX
OF RECIPES

ALPHABETICAL INDEX
OF INGREDIENTS

All the photographs are by Academia Barilla except:
©123RF: timer image
©iStockphoto: pages 2, 4, 5, 7, 8, 11, 123, 125, 126, 128
Joff Lee/Getty Images: cover and back cover

ACADEMIA BARILLA
ITALIAN GASTRONOMIC AMBASSADOR TO THE WORLD

In the heart of Parma, recognized as one of the most prestigious capitals of cuisine, the Barilla Center stands in the middle of Barilla's historical headquarters, now hosting Academia Barilla's modern structure. Founded in 2004 with the aim of affirming the role of Italian culinary arts, protecting the regional gastronomic heritage, defending it from imitations and counterfeits and to valorize the great tradition of Italian cooking, Academia Barilla is where great professionalism and unique competences in the world of cuisine meet. The institution organizes cooking courses for those passionate about food culture, offering services dedicated to the operators in the sector and proposing products of unparalleled quality. Academia Barilla was awarded the "Business-Culture Prize" for its promotional activities regarding gastronomic culture and Italian creativity in the world. Our headquarters were designed to meet the educational needs in the field of food preparation and has the multimedia tools necessary to host large events: around an extraordinary gastronomic auditorium, there is an internal restaurant, a multisensory laboratory and various classrooms equipped with the most modern technology. In our Gastronomic Library we conserve over 10,000 volumes regarding specific topics and an unusual collection of historical menus and printed materials on the culinary arts: the library's enormous cultural heritage is available online and allows anyone to access hundreds of digitalized historical texts. This forward thinking organization and the presence of an internationally renowned team of professors guarantee a wide rage of courses, able to satisfy the needs of both catering professionals as well as simple cuisine enthusiasts. Academia Barilla also organizes cultural events and initiatives for highlighting culinary sciences open to the public, with the participation of experts, chefs and food critics. It also promotes the "Cinema Award", especially for short-length films dedicated to Italian food traditions.

www.academiabarilla.it

WHITE STAR PUBLISHERS

WS White Star Publishers® is a registered trademark
property of De Agostini Libri S.p.A.

© 2013 De Agostini Libri S.p.A.
Via G. da Verrazano, 15
28100 Novara, Italy
www.whitestar.it - www.deagostini.it

ISBN 978-88-544-0771-8
1 2 3 4 5 6   17 16 15 14 13

Printed in China

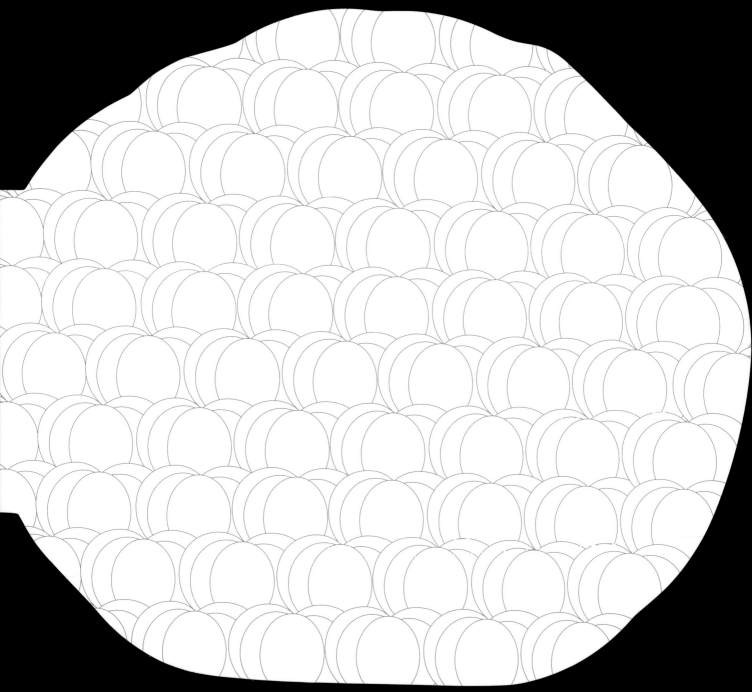

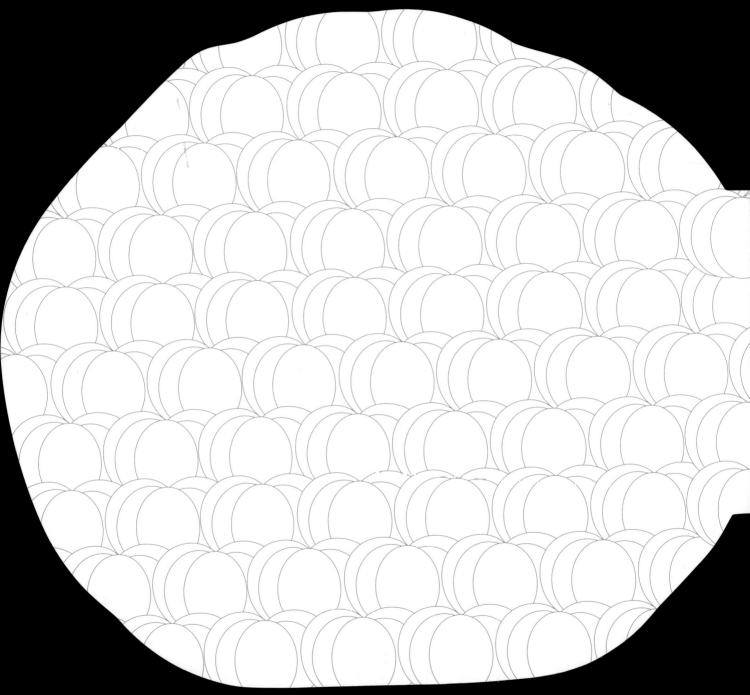